Canterbury

a pocket miscellany

Kathryn Bedford

First published 2012

The History Press
The Mill, Brimscombe Port
Stroud, Gloucestershire, GL5 2QG
www.thehistorypress.co.uk

© Kathryn Bedford, 2012

The right of Kathryn Bedford to be identified as the Author
of this work has been asserted in accordance with the
Copyrights, Designs and Patents Act 1988.

All rights reserved. No part of this book may be reprinted
or reproduced or utilised in any form or by any electronic,
mechanical or other means, now known or hereafter invented,
including photocopying and recording, or in any information
storage or retrieval system, without the permission in writing
from the Publishers.

British Library Cataloguing in Publication Data.
A catalogue record for this book is available from the British Library.

ISBN 978 0 7524 6885 3

Typesetting and origination by The History Press
Manufacturing managed by Jellyfish Print Solutions Ltd
Printed in Great Britain

Coat of Arms

The golden leopard on a red background, and the crown above the shield, indicate that Canterbury is a royal city, a distinction it has been granted since at least the sixth century.

*

The three black choughs (medium-sized birds with red legs and beak which are closely related to the jackdaw) are from the arms attributed to Archbishop Thomas Becket: they symbolise the city's religious role as a place of pilgrimage.

*

The motto, *Ave Mater Anglia*, means 'Hail, Mother of England'.

Contents

Definition of the Name

Canterbury is located on the site of the old Roman town of Durovernum Cantiacorum, a name which referred to the area's previous role as an Iron Age fort, but the name was changed in the sixth century. The modern name derives from the Old English *Cantwareburh*, meaning the city (or court) of the men of Kent.

Grid Reference

Church Lane – 51° 16' 36.05" N, 1° 4' 29.16" E

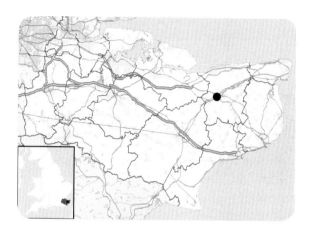

First Appearance on a Map

Due to Canterbury's role as a cathedral city and major pilgrimage site, the city appears on a number of very early world maps, including the Hereford Mapa Mundi, *c.* 1300, where it is represented by a generic building intended to represent the cathedral. However, such maps were not geographically accurate.

It was not until the 1610 'Map of the County of Kent' by William Camden that an accurate representation of the city's location was produced. Camden included an illustration of the city walls as well as the cathedral in his depiction.

The city itself had been mapped out in 1588 by William Smith, but there are sufficient inaccuracies in his version to indicate that he was working from someone else's plan and had never visited the city himself.

Street Names

Many of Canterbury's streets are named after saints or the three orders of monks that lived within its bounds, reflecting the city's religious role, but there are others with more varied origins:

Black Griffin Lane – Named after the pub on the corner, itself a possible reference to Chaucer's *Knight's Tale*.

Cow Lane – A man called Smith used to drive his cows along this street to the dairy and back twice a day. Since livestock had right of way, all the other traffic had to stop to let them pass, and the name developed partly as a reminder to avoid the lane at those times.

Duck Lane – Unlike Cow Lane, this is not a reference to the animal. The name grew out of the word *ducere* (to lead) from the Latin phrase for 'leading to the river', which is what the lane does.

Old Ruttington Lane – With Saxon origins, and over 1,000 years old, this is one of the oldest thoroughfares in the country and one of the oldest street names in existence. It means 'street of the royal personage' because Queen Bertha passed along it every day to worship at St Martin's church.

Orange Street – A reference to William of Orange, of 'William and Mary' fame, this is the only road in the city to be named after a monarch.

Pound Lane – Rather than relating to money, this was where the pound, a secure holding area for stray animals, was located.

Roper Road – Originally called Hanover Place, the name of this road was changed during the First World War following a petition by residents to substitute an English name for the original German one.

Wards

The city of Canterbury is administered as part of Kent's larger district of Canterbury, which also includes Herne Bay and Whitstable. The majority of the city falls within three wards:

Westgate – Contains most of the older parts of the city, including the area inside the city walls.

Northgate – A comparatively high proportion of families and commuters.

St Stephen's – A particularly student-centric area with much of the population in their teens and twenties, though most of Canterbury is full of students in term time.

However, parts of the city extend into three more wards:

Barton – Extremely diverse. Some very wealthy areas, but also has a higher than average proportion of people on benefits.

Wincheap – Has few features to distinguish it from the other wards. Lots of students during term, especially in some areas.

Harbledown – The ward with the most countryside and the highest proportion of senior citizens. It also has a large Jewish population.

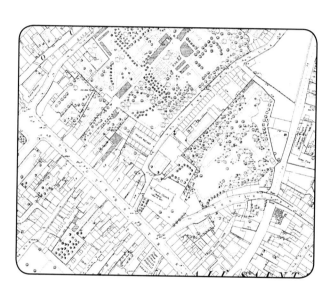

Distance From...

Place	Miles	Km
Ayers Rock, Northern Territory	9,911	15,950
Brussels, Belgium	146	235
Centre of the Earth	3,975	6,397
Death Valley, USA	5,313	8,550
Eiffel Tower, Paris	176	283
Frankfurt, Germany	342	551
Glasgow, Scotland	385	620
Hong Kong, China	5,940	9,560
Istanbul, Turkey	1,499	2,412
Jerusalem, Israel	2,188	3,521
The Kremlin, Russia	1,514	2,436
Lima, Peru	6,369	10,250
The Moon (average)	238,857	384,403
Niagara Falls, North America	3,615	5,818
Osaka, Japan	5,886	9,473
The Panama Canal	5,331	8,580
Queenstown, New Zealand	11,719	18,860
Reykjavik, Iceland	1,215	1,955
Syracuse, Sicily	1,204	1,937
The Taj Mahal, India	4,228	6,804
Ural Mountains, Russia	2,236	3,599
Vatican City	843	1,356
Washington DC, USA	3,720	5,986
Xanthi, Greece	1,327	2,136
Yellowstone National Park	4,649	7,482
Zurich, Switzerland	547	880

Town Twinnings

Reims, France – Twinned since 1962

Reims, like Canterbury, is a centre of Christianity within its country; traditionally all French kings were crowned in its cathedral.

There is a strong and active connection between the two cities: for example, every year delegations from Canterbury take part in the Reims festival, which celebrates the life of Joan of Arc. There have also been a number of cycle rides between the two cities along the Via Francigena, which goes from Canterbury to Rome via Reims.

International Places with the Same Name

Canterbury, Waitaha, New Zealand
Canterbury is an administrative region which shares a religious connection with its namesake; the area was settled from 1850 in an attempt to establish a colony which would be sponsored by the Church of England.

Canterbury, New Hampshire, United States
The Shaker village founded here in 1792 was turned into a museum for the sect in 1969. The village has been designated a National Historic Landmark since 1993.

Canterbury, Connecticut, United States
The location, in 1832, of the first racially integrated classroom in the United States – which led to outrage and boycotting of the school by some white families.

Canterbury, New Brunswick, Canada
A small village, originally settled by royalist Americans fleeing the USA after the War of Independence.

Canterbury, Melbourne and Canterbury, Sydney, Australia
Both of Australia's largest cities have administrative regions named Canterbury.

Timeline

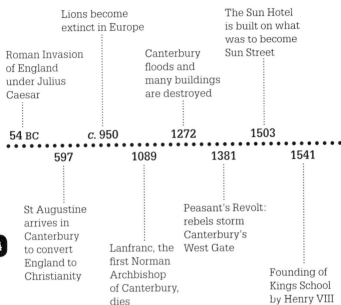

Lions become extinct in Europe

Roman Invasion of England under Julius Caesar

The Sun Hotel is built on what was to become Sun Street

Canterbury floods and many buildings are destroyed

54 BC   *c.* 950   1272   1503

597   1089   1381   1541

St Augustine arrives in Canterbury to convert England to Christianity

Lanfranc, the first Norman Archbishop of Canterbury, dies

Peasant's Revolt: rebels storm Canterbury's West Gate

Founding of Kings School by Henry VIII

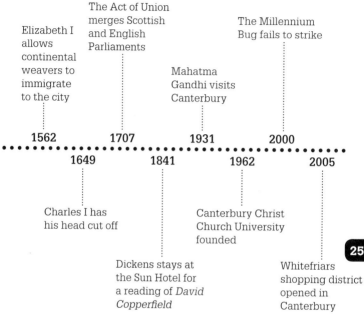

Elizabeth I allows continental weavers to immigrate to the city

1562

The Act of Union merges Scottish and English Parliaments

1707

Mahatma Gandhi visits Canterbury

1931

The Millennium Bug fails to strike

2000

1649

Charles I has his head cut off

1841

Dickens stays at the Sun Hotel for a reading of *David Copperfield*

1962

Canterbury Christ Church University founded

2005

Whitefriars shopping district opened in Canterbury

Seasons

Averages in recent years

	Spring	Summer	Autumn	Winter
Temperature (°C)	10.04	17.25	14.32	5.45
Rainfall (mm)	132.69	138.03	160.2	130.54
Wind speed (mph)	0.99	0.62	0.89	1.03

Extremes in recent years

Highest temperature: 33.6 °C, on 19 July 2006

Lowest temperature: -9.5 °C, on 10 January 2009

Wettest day: 29.0mm rainfall, on 24 May 2008

Wettest month: 110.5mm rainfall, in August 2006

Driest month: 0.0 mm rainfall, in April 2007

Day in the Life

0630 – First tee off at the golf course

0800 – Morning prayers in the cathedral

0900 – Shops open on the High Street and business begins

1000 – First river tour of the day

1100 – Lectures underway at the universities

1300 – Lunch available at the Weavers' Cottage Tearoom

1500 – French language service in the cathedral

1600 – Last entry to both the Roman and Canterbury museums

1730 – Evensong in the cathedral

1930 – Performance starts at the Marlowe Theatre

2000 – Walking tour of Canterbury's haunted buildings sets out

0200 – Canterbury's biggest nightclub, BaaBars, closes

How Many Times a Year...

...do services take place in the cathedral? **2,000**

...do walking tours detail the city's haunted past? **104**

... do the Canterbury Council Committee hold a meeting? **9**

... is *District Life*, the Canterbury City Council's local newsletter, published? **2**

How many...

...tourists visit Canterbury? **30 million**

...people yearly visit the council website? **886,400**

...books were issued by University of Kent Library? **500,000**

...people visit the public library per year? **140,000**

...people attend the Canterbury Festival? **70,000**

...hours of volunteer work by University of Kent students? **36,000**

...number of graduates of Canterbury Christ Church? **2,299**

...league matches are played at home by Canterbury City FC? **15**

Demographics

Population
Total population of the district – **135,278**
Total population of the city – **43,432**
Proportion of male residents – **47.8 per cent**
Proportion of female residents – **52.2 per cent**
Adults with a higher education qualification – **27 per cent**
Average age of residents – **37.1**
Male life expectancy – **77.5**
Female life expectancy – **85.0**

Households
Total number of households – **17,536**
One-person households – **35 per cent**
Couples – **39 per cent**
Lone parents – **10 per cent**
Other – **15 per cent**

% of the population by age

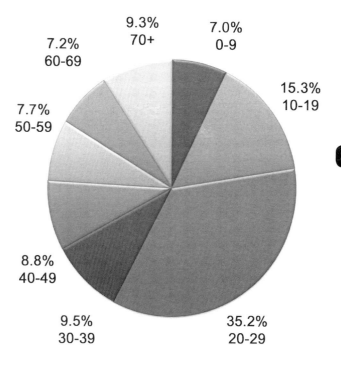

Ethnicity

White – **95 per cent**
Asian – **1.8 per cent**
Black – **0.7 per cent**

Foreign-born residents – **11.6 per cent**

Employment

Proportion of population at working age – **72.5 per cent**
Proportion unemployed – **2.7 per cent**
Total number who work in the city – **18,200**
Proportion of male workers – **47.6 per cent**
Proportion of female workers – **52.4 per cent**

% of the population by religion

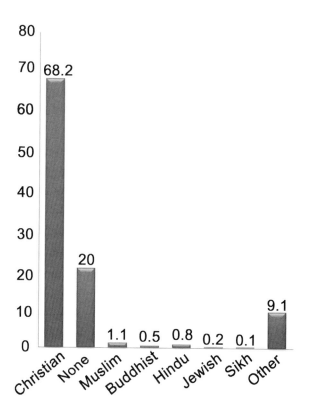

Strange Statistics

500+ – The number of jars of sweets at the Sugar Boy sweet shop.

460 – The number of patients treated by Dane John's hospital in the first year of the First World War. Only one died.

1.5 million – The number of bricks in Bell Harry Tower of the cathedral; it was the first brick building to be constructed in the city since Roman times.

80ft – The original height of the castle's keep, the third oldest keep in England. The walls were 14.5ft thick.

21 – The number of towers originally on the city's wall; there were also eight gates. Almost half of these survive.

11 – The number of nurseries in the city centre growing plants for sale in 1930/31.

2 – The number of competing cinemas which opened in Canterbury on the same day, 5 August 1933.

16ft – The height of Oast Houses, common around Canterbury and throughout Kent. They are topped by roofs that stretch to 20ft.

12 – The number of parish churches in Canterbury, with three more in the suburbs. There used to be a further five, but these have been demolished.

Famous for…

The cathedral – The most famous and iconic building in Canterbury, but difficult to see from within the city itself because the precincts are largely enclosed. It is the premier cathedral within the Church of England and one of the oldest churches in the country.

The Holy Maid of Kent – A servant girl who became a member of St Sepulchre's Nunnery, Canterbury. She claimed the gift of prophesy and spoke out against Henry VIII's divorce from Catherine of Aragon. Unsurprisingly she was executed, being hanged in 1534.

Archbishop – The leading cleric of the English Church. There have been over 100 Archbishops of Canterbury since St Augustine originally arrived to convert England. They have included saints, cardinals, politicians and theologians.

Christopher Marlowe – This Elizabethan playwright is ubiquitous in the city, and is referenced in street names, a university building, a café, and the three Marlowe Theatres that have existed over the years. The clock tower at the east end of the high street is all that remains of the church in which he was christened.

Chaucer's *Canterbury Tales* – One of the first works of literature in English, the *Tales* recount the stories told by a varied group of pilgrims travelling to Canterbury to worship at the shrine of Thomas Becket.

The Weavers' House – A splendid and much photographed Tudor building that was the centre of the weaving trade; the industry sustained the city after the loss of income from pilgrims following the Reformation. What can be seen is mostly late sixteenth-century, but parts of it date back to the twelfth.

Canterbury muslin – Invented by John Callaway in 1787, Canterbury muslin was a very fine blend of cotton and silk which could be created on a modified form of the Spinning Jenny machine. It temporarily restored Canterbury's weaving industry, which had been hit by the Industrial Revolution.

Canterbury Gospels – A sixth-century illuminated manuscript of the gospels supposedly brought to England by St Augustine. Now owned by Corpus Christi College, Cambridge, the book is occasionally loaned to the city for special occasions.

Infamous for...

Thomas More's head – Following his execution by Henry VIII, Thomas More's daughter stole his severed head (which was on display in London). She hid it in a box under her bed covered in flower petals until she was able to have it buried in St Dunstan's church, Canterbury, which was her husband's parish church.

Dr Hewlett Johnson – He became known as 'The Red Dean of Canterbury' – a role he held for over thirty years (from 1931-63) – for his ongoing support of Soviet Communism. He was accused of 'spreading defeatist propaganda' for supporting the Soviets despite the fact that Britain was at war with Germany.

Canterbury Barracks – The threat of invasion from France in the eighteenth century led to the building of a number of barracks around the city in the vicinity of Military Road. By the nineteenth century they covered more area than the city itself and were not fully demolished until after the Second World War.

The murder of Archbishop Becket

By far the most infamous historical event associated with Canterbury is the death of Saint Thomas Becket in 1170. Becket had been a close associate of Henry II but – following his appointment to Canterbury – they fell out. Four knights took up the king's apparent challenge to rid him of 'this turbulent priest', and first tried to arrest Becket before killing him – by the unusual method of cutting off the top of his head. Eyewitness accounts include that by the scholar John of Salisbury, who hid behind a pillar in the cathedral and saw the whole thing.

The knights were never arrested or fined, but Henry II chose to undertake a pilgrimage to his friend's tomb to atone.

A wonderful painting representing the whole story can be seen in the Canterbury Museum.

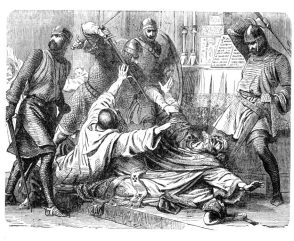

Quotations in Literature

'From every shire end of England to Canterbury they wend, the holy blissful martyr for to seek.'
Chaucer, *Canterbury Tales*

'I seemed to be sustained and led on by my fanciful picture of my mother in her youth, before I came into the world… I have associated it, ever since, with the sunny street of Canterbury, dozing as it were in the hot light; and with the sight of its old houses and gateways, and the stately, grey cathedral, with the rooks sailing round the towers.'
Charles Dickens, *David Copperfield*

'Along one side lay the cathedral with its great central tower, and Philip, who knew as yet nothing of beauty, felt when he looked at it a troubling delight which he could not understand.'
William Somerset Maugham, *Of Human Bondage*

Quotations in Histories

'The appearance of the city of Canterbury, from whatever part you approach it, is beautiful, and equals the most sanguine expectation.'
Edward Hasted, *The History and Topography of the County of Kent*

'…its antiquity seems to be its greatest beauty. The houses are truly ancient, and the many ruins of churches, chapels, oratories, and smaller cells of religious people, makes the place look like a general ruin a little recovered.'
Daniel Defoe, *Tour Through the Whole Island of Great Britain*

'Grouped round its dominating church the city huddled as if it sought protection against progress and modernity. Bell Harry in his beauty seemed a giant lighthouse pointing heavenwards.'
R.B. Cunningham Graham, *Redeemed* **(describing Joseph Conrad's funeral)**

Quotations by Famous People

'This evening I go to Canterbury – having got tired of Margate – I was not right in my head when I came – at Canterbury I hope the Remembrance of Chaucer will set me forward like a billiard ball.'
Letter by John Keats

'There is no lovelier place in the world than Canterbury – that I say with my hand on my heart as I sit in Florence – and I have seen Venice too.'
Letter by Virginia Woolf

'…an old, ugly medieval sort of town, not mended by large modern English barracks at the one end and a dismal dry Railway Station at the other end of the oldish thing. There is no trace of poetry about it… Happily I was too tired, and it was too late, to look out for the celebrated cathedral.'
Letter by Karl Marx

Headlines from Newspapers

'Orlando Bloomed at an Early Stage' (20 December 2001)

Following the huge success of the film version of *The Lord of the Rings: The Fellowship of the Ring* much was made in Kent of Orlando Bloom's connection to Canterbury. In this article his old teacher discusses his school acting experiences.

Aged 14, he took on a lead part in Sandy Wilson's *The Boyfriend*, playing the aged Lord Brockhurst: 'He played the 70-year old man wonderfully: the posture, the mannerisms. He got a massive ovation.'

'Landmark New Theatre Will Put Canterbury Centre Stage' (17 August 2011)

In spite of local hostility to the new building, business and political leaders are enthusiastic that the redevelopment will promote tourism as well as encourage people to move to the area.

'Within the sound of the bells of Canterbury Cathedral, the finishing touches are being put to a significantly more state-of-the-art landmark… The new theatre, designed by the architect Keith Williams, will bring a welcome cultural fillip to the city.'

Museums and Galleries

Museum of Canterbury – Housed in a 1373 poor priests' hospital, much of the original structure of which can still be seen.

Roman Museum – Shows Roman mosaics *in situ*, and reproductions of a Roman house. Lots of activities for children.

The Canterbury Tales – A very famous attraction telling a selection of Chaucer's stories in an immersive, medieval style environment.

Pilgrim Hospital – Founded in 1180 as one of a number of hospices set up for pilgrims, the parts not open to the public are still used as a home by retired clergy and notable parishioners.

Sidney Cooper Gallery – At the west end of the High Street. The gallery is part of Christ Church University and exhibits local artists. Entrance is free.

Westgate Museum – Housed in the Westgate itself, and detailing the building's use as a defensive structure and prison.

World Heritage Site

Canterbury Cathedral, the ruins of St Augustine's Abbey and St Martin's church were collectively made a UNESCO World Heritage Site in 1988, only two years after the first set of sites were announced.

The cathedral's Chapter House, off the cloisters, is the largest of its kind in England.

St Martin's church is the oldest church in the English-speaking world which is still in use. It dates from before the arrival of St Augustine and was the regular church of Queen Bertha, the French wife of King Ethelbert.

In its heyday, the church of St Augustine's Abbey was of similar size to the cathedral.

After the Dissolution of the Monasteries, part of the Abbey was converted into a palace intended for the use of Anne of Cleves, before Henry VIII decided that she was too ugly and divorced her.

In the Domesday Book the lands belonging to the cathedral and St Augustine's Abbey together covered nearly half of Kent.

Ecclesiæ Cathedralis et Metropoliticæ
Christi Cantuariensis, facies australis.

Oldest

Conquest House (on Palace Street) – The oldest house in the city. The four knights who murdered Becket met in the undercroft of this building before going to the cathedral.

King's Bridge (by the Old Weavers' House) – Has been widened over the years but the original part was built in 1134, making this the oldest functioning road bridge in England.

The gap between one side of King's Bridge and the adjoining building is the remains of the city's oldest public toilet, essentially a wooden plank over a drop to the river. It was closed shortly after it opened because a woman fell in and died.

Greyfriars – What remains of the once extensive complex is the oldest surviving example of Franciscan architecture in the country. It survived the Dissolution of the Monasteries because it was the only bridge across the river at the time.

West Gate – Built in 1380, it is the earliest known fortification in England that was built specifically to be defended by guns.

Award Winners

While Canterbury is best known for its multiplicity of medieval and Tudor buildings, some modern structures have received acknowledgement from the architectural community. In recent years Canterbury's higher education institutions have been particularly successful:

Canterbury College redevelopment – South East Building Excellence Award, 2009

Augustine House, Christ Church University – South East Building Excellence Award, 2010

Jarman Building, University of Kent – Royal Institute of British Architects Award, 2010

Above the Shop Fronts

When walking around Canterbury city centre it is always worth looking up: the modern glass shop windows at ground level give way to old and decorated frontages by the first floor. There are a particularly large number of medieval and Tudor beamed frontages, but other examples to watch out for include:

Queen Elizabeth's Guest Chamber – Has a grand frontage with relief moulding. It was originally an inn for pilgrims but is more famous as the location of a meeting between the Virgin Queen and her admirer Francis, Duke of Anjou, in 1573.

No. 8 High Street (now Past Times) – Apparently uninteresting from the front, the back of this building has exposed medieval beams. It is interesting because when it was first constructed in the fifteenth century the street layout was different so that what can now be seen is actually the side of the building.

Debenhams on Guildhall Street – This has a far more modern frontage, but still unusual. The front of the first and second floors consists entirely of Art-Deco-style stained glass windows, probably from the later 1920s or early 1930s.

Doorways

St John Boy's House (at the end of Palace Street) – This precarious looking house, with its famous tilted doorway, is one of the most photographed buildings in the city. The door was shifted due to a chimney alteration and the angle has been made more extreme to encourage tourists.

Christ Church (Sanctuary) Gate – The main entrance to the cathedral precinct, and one of the most iconic structures in the city. This impressive gatehouse, which dominates the surrounding streets, was built by Henry VII to commemorate the death of his eldest son, Arthur.

Side door to Blackfriars – A half-height door that can only be seen from the river. Its small size is a result of a rise in water levels which necessitated a rise in the river bank to accommodate it. The river tours joke that it was made that size because all the monks were hobbits.

Roper Gate – On St Dunstan's Street, this is the former entrance to the home of William Roper, son-in-law and biographer to Thomas More. The house in which More's head was kept briefly before its internment.

Hidden Faces

All around Canterbury can be found carved faces, demons and grotesques if you look out for them. Examples include:

No. 8 Palace Street – A thirteenth-century building with two hermaphrodite wood carvings which show both breasts and a moustache.

Prêt a Manger in Mercery Lane – Has a set of two more modern devil figures, one happy and one grumpy.

Antique shop on Palace Street – Amongst the carvings lining the roof is a face and there are two harpies supporting a jettied second floor.

Cathedral – As could be expected, there are a huge number of grotesques attached to the cathedral. Listing them all would be futile, but look particularly above door lintels. A famous pair of grotesques pulling faces, one covering its ears with its tongue stuck out and the other holding its mouth open, can be found at the west end.

Tea shop at the end of Burgate – A demon holding its breasts adorns the door in a pose that is quite typical for this kind of figure.

All Saints Lane – One of the doors in the row of fifteenth-century terraced houses has a pair of faces carved into the lintel. The other doors on this row have simple plant forms instead.

Parks and Green Spaces

Dane John Gardens – The name comes from the Norman *donjon* (castle mound), as the original castle, built following 1066, was on what is now the Memorial Mound. Alderman Simmons funded and laid out the gardens and had the memorial made for his tomb.

Westgate Gardens – Surrounding Tower House, which was itself built around one of the bastions of the medieval wall, and stretching quite some way along the river, this is a beautiful space. It contains a medieval archway, which was probably moved from St Augustine's Abbey.

Abbot's Mill Garden – A popular but hard-to-find space next to the river. The Mill itself burnt down in 1936 – the fire lasted two days. Fire-fighters were distracted partway through when the pub next door caught fire too, and had to divide their efforts. The pub still stands and can be seen from the gardens.

Butterfly Garden – A small space off Pound Lane designed to encourage butterflies and give people a space to feed the ducks on the river.

Greyfriars Garden – Slightly out of the way and very quiet. Includes a wild flower meadow and access to the Greyfriars Chapel, which is open to the public.

War Memorial Gardens – Contains a stone from the destroyed medieval cloth hall at Ypres to commemorate the members of the voluntary Canterbury regiment who died in the three Battles of Ypres in the First World War.

Flora and Fauna

Apple Trees – The Mill Garden used to be an orchard for the Blackfriars, and in memory of its Dominican past several 'religiously themed' apple trees were planted there in 2005. Varieties include Chorister Boy, Christmas Pearman and Easter Orange.

Oak Trees – Oak makes up the majority of the Blean, the woods surrounding the city. Unusually, it is not grown for timber but was coppiced for use in the tanning industry until the 1950s.

Oriental Plane Tree – One of the oldest such trees in Britain can be found in Westgate Gardens. It is believed to be over 200 years old.

Butterflies – As well as having their own garden, the area has a connection with these creatures through the nature reserve in the Blean, which is home to the rare fritillary butterfly.

Job Sectors

Sector	Employees
Education	12,200
Wholesale and retail trade	11,000
Human health and social work activities	10,500
Accommodation and food-service activities	3,900
Public administration and defence	3,300
Professional, scientific and technical activities	3,000
Administrative and support service activities	2,700
Construction	2,300
Manufacturing	2,100
Transportation and storage	1,300
Information and communication	1,200
Financial and insurance activities	1,100
Arts, entertainment and recreation	1,100
Primary industries	700
Real-estate activities	600
Other service activities	1,900

No. of Employees

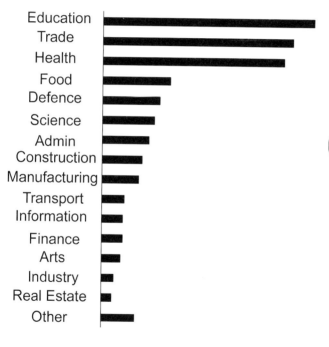

Largest Employers

Employer	Employees
University of Kent	1,846
Canterbury Christ Church University	1,437
Nurse Plus and Carer Plus (UK) Ltd (which supplies temporary nursing and care staff)	712
Robert Brett & Sons, Ltd Mineral extraction and civil engineering	685
Motorline Holdings Ltd (a motor dealership)	389

Historic Jobs

Weaving – An initial group of eighteen foreign silk weavers settled in Canterbury in AD 1562. By AD 1634 there were 900 – and by 1676 that figure had grown to nearly 2,500. The industry was killed off in the eighteenth century by the Industrial Revolution.

Hop-picking – As with the rest of Kent, Canterbury was surrounded by hop farms which provided much of the work in the area. The hop harvest would often see three generations of the same family working side by side. One woman, known as 'Granny' Roberts, picked hops for over seventy-two years.

Tannery – The site of Canterbury's St Mildred's Tannery is even older than that of the cathedral. It produced very high quality leather, which was used on the Coronation coach of Edward VII, and in Rolls-Royces, Ferraris, and the Houses of Parliament.

Milling – There have been eight mills in Canterbury over the years. The last watermill in the city to work for trade was Barton Mill, which was finally destroyed by fire in 2004; some parts of it have been converted into housing.

Butchery – One man who worked in a Canterbury slaughterhouse described the process: he used a mallet to stun the pigs, but was put off the job by having to hold the front legs of calves while cutting their heads off.

Born

Christopher Marlowe (*b.* 1564)

The son of a Canterbury shoemaker, Marlowe was a Tudor playwright who outshone, and was an inspiration to, Shakespeare. The less public side of his career involved using his theatrical connections to spy for Elizabeth I in Europe. He died in mysterious circumstances during a pub brawl in Deptford, London.

Thomas Sidney Cooper (*b.* 1803)

A landscape painter especially known for his sheep and cattle, leading to the epithet 'Cows Cooper'. The art school he set up in Canterbury still exists in the form of the University of Creative Arts.

Sir Freddie Laker (*b.* 1922)

An early airline entrepreneur who began working in aviation during the Second World War. In 1966 he set up his own airline, Laker Airways, which was one of the first to use the 'no frills' business model which has proved so successful for companies like easyJet.

Fiona Phillips (*b.* 1961)

A television presenter best known for her long-running position on *GMTV*. Initially appearing as the entertainment correspondent, she was promoted to main anchor in 1997. She has also appeared as a regular panellist on *Loose Women*.

The Tragicall Hiftoy of
the Life and Death
of Doctor Fauftus.

With new Additions.

Written by *Ch. Mar.*

Died

Bartholomew, Lord Badlesmere (*d.* 1322)

He supported Thomas, Earl of Lancaster against Edward II. It was the imprisonment of his wife and children – after they refused to admit Queen Isabella to Leeds Castle in 1321 – that sparked a civil war. He was captured only a year later and was hanged, drawn and quartered at the Blean, just outside Canterbury. His head was displayed in Burgate.

Protestant Martyrs (*d.* 1555)

During the reign of Queen Mary, ten woman and thirty-one men were executed in Canterbury for refusing to renounce their Protestant beliefs. Four of these men – John Bland, John Frankesh, Nicholas Sheterden and Humphrey Middleton – appear collectively in *Foxe's Book of Martyrs* as the 'Canterbury Martyrs'. Apparently they 'resigned themselves with Christian fortitude, fervently praying that God would receive them into his heavenly kingdom.'

Joseph Conrad (*d.* 1924)

Regarded as one of the greatest novelists in the English canon, his most widely read works are *Lord Jim*, *Nostromo* and *Heart of Darkness*, which was the inspiration for the film *Apocalypse Now*. He died of a heart attack and was buried in Canterbury under his original Polish name, Korzeniowski.

Blue Plaques

James Simmons (1741-1807)
James lived at 24 High Street, Canterbury from 1802 to 1807. Simmons was responsible for transforming Canterbury into a 'Georgian' town through his official roles as MP, Alderman and Mayor. He also founded the *Kentish Gazette* newspaper which has remained in production ever since.

William Sealy Gosset (1876-1937)
The statistician who developed the student 't' distribution test, fundamental to modern statistics. He was born and raised at No. 6 St Martin's Hill, Canterbury, and has been referred to as the 'Faraday of statistics'. Gosset developed the test while working in quality control for Guinness.

Count Louis Zborowski (1895-1924)
An early racing driver and car engineer who constructed two of his *Chitty Chitty Bang Bang* cars in a workshop at No. 16 St Radigund's Street, Canterbury, between 1921 and 1922. During his racing career he drove for both Aston Martin and Bugatti, eventually being fatally injured while driving for the Mercedes team in the Italian Grand Prix.

Professor Cyril Northcote Parkinson (1909-1993)
Lived at No. 36 Harkness Drive, Canterbury from 1988 to 1993. Parkinson was an historian and author who created the concept known as 'Parkinson's Law' – work expands so as to fill the time available for its completion.

Local Characters

Francis Bennett-Goldney – Mayor and later MP for Canterbury, but a very dubious character. He embezzled many of the city's historic documents and is even suspected of being involved in the theft of the Irish Crown Jewels.

H. Hopper – A baker at No. 80 Wincheap Street from the 1930s to '60s who became known for baking the longest loaf in the world. It took four people to carry it.

River Tour Guides – Seen all around the more touristy parts of the city but especially by the Weavers' House. Holding oars and encouraging passers-by to take to the river, these young men are synonymous with summer in Canterbury.

"THE LONGEST LOAF IN THE WORLD." baked by Mr. H. Hopper, of Wincheap Street.

85

Criminals and their Crimes

Robert Cushman – The man who organised the purchase of the *Mayflower* in which the Pilgrim Fathers travelled to America was held in Westgate prison for a time because of his religious views, along with a number of America's other Founding Fathers. He did not travel on the *Mayflower* himself, but eventually made it to America in 1621 – only to return shortly afterwards to encourage others to follow. He died of plague.

Debtor's Despair

In 1733, an unnamed actor imprisoned in the Westgate wrote the following poem:

A place there is, of ancient date

Entering the city, called Westgate.

Here felons lodge, and each poor debtor

Who cannot pay for lodging better…

…No pity's shown, but there must lie

Perchance until the wretches die

James – In June 1793, the *Kentish Gazette* reported the repeated attempts by a fifteen- or sixteen-year-old petty thief to escape from his imprisonment in the Westgate. He had even succeeded in breaking the iron manacles on his wrists and ankles. When stronger restraints were put in place, he declared to the guards that he would carry on trying.

George Bennett – Escaped from Westgate prison on New Year's Day, 1828. He managed to use the flag and the flag pole on the roof to lower himself over the side. This option was not available to later offenders, as the flag pole blew down in 1832.

Mr Woods – A popular butcher on Sun Street in the early 1960s. However, inspectors found his sausages to be dusty and dirty and demanded that the shop close. Woods maintained that he had been sabotaged by a member of his staff.

Fictional Characters

David Copperfield – Dickens's leading man grew up in Canterbury. A number of other characters in the book were actually based on real Canterbury residents. For example, Agnes Wakefield was named after the daughter of a local solicitor and is commemorated in the sixteenth-century House of Agnes on St Dunstan's Street.

Rupert Bear – Created by Mary Tourtel, who was born in and died at Canterbury. Rupert first appeared in the *Daily Express* in 1920, and his adventures have continued to the present day with a variety of illustrators. Rupert has a whole room dedicated to him in Canterbury Museum; the exhibit includes 'the Frog Chorus', from the animated Rupert film; this was a number three hit in the charts of 1984.

Bagpuss, The Clangers and Ivor the Engine – These, and a number of other well-loved children's television characters, were created by Peter Firmin and Oliver Postgate from their studio just outside Canterbury. Although only thirteen episodes of *Bagpuss* were made, the show came first in a 1999 BBC poll of the nation's favourite children's show, and fourth in the 2001 Channel 4 poll, *The Greatest Kids' TV Shows*.

Ghosts

The housekeeper **Ellen Blean** is said to haunt St Dunstan's Street and the Bishop's Finger Inn every Friday night. She poisoned two people (the canon she worked for and his mistress) when she discovered they were having an affair, disappearing soon after. Many years later her body was discovered walled up in a nearby building.

Another lascivious canon was murdered by the uncle of his mistress, the servant **Nell Cook**. Nell's ghost has been seen walking the grounds of the cathedral, stooped with regret. Her story inspired the story *The Ghost* in Richard Barham's 1840 collection, *The Ingoldsby Legends*.

The cathedral is allegedly a hive of paranormal activity: alongside Nell, it is home to the ghosts of a nun and **Simon of Sudbury**, a fourteenth-century archbishop. The sound of spectral plainchant has also been reported.

Simon of Sudbury apparently has an active afterlife, since he is also suspected of being the ghost seen at **Sudbury Tower** on Pound Lane. The spectre haunts a Tower bedroom, apparently tucking the occupant in at night.

I Love…

The cathedral – The beauty of the building has led many residents and tourists to fall in love with the cathedral. The single most recognisable building in the city has provided a geographical and economic heart to the city over the centuries, as well as an aesthetic one.

Small size – Canterbury is a very small city: the entirety of the walled area can be explored in a single day. As a result, it is often characterised by residents as 'a large village or town' in which everyone knows each other and in which everyone is friendly, rather than a stereotypical city.

Streets around the cathedral – The collection of small streets surrounding the cathedral's precincts are a favourite of most visitors to Canterbury as they are full of character and provide an unusual shopping experience.

Clean river – The River Stour (a name meaning 'angry' or 'fast-flowing' river, although it is now thoroughly tamed) and its canals are beautifully clear. Such cleanliness provides a good habitat for wildlife, including an impressive quantity of plant-life.

I Hate…

Local satisfaction with Canterbury is almost universal.

When asked what they disliked about the city, most residents had difficulty supplying an answer. The only point of contention is the design of the new Marlowe Theatre, which is felt to be of a size and design which is out-of-keeping with the character of the surrounding buildings.

Favourite Scene

Least Favourite Scene

Rebellious Canterbury

Peasants' Revolt (1381) – Canterbury was a focus of the rebels' activities. They broke into the newly constructed Westgate looking for Archbishop Sudbury, the Lord Chancellor, who was particularly associated with the unpopular Poll Tax. He was eventually found at the Tower of London and executed.

Jack Cade's rebellion (1450) – The city of Canterbury was made a county corporate – in effect, a separate county from Kent – in 1461, as thanks for the city not having supported the rebels. However, although officials were loyal to the Crown, the city itself was at the centre of the rebellion.

Christmas riots (1647) – Following the initial phase of the Civil War, rioting broke out in Canterbury on Christmas Day when the Mayor tried to enforce Parliament's ban on celebrating Christmas. This riot sparked the Counter Revolution which sought to restore Charles I to the throne.

More recent and peaceful protests include:

CND March (1980) – This was an early example of the 1980s resurgence of interest in nuclear disarmament. A 4-mile march ended with speeches in the Dane John Gardens.

Fathers 4 Justice (2009) – The group dressed as Father Christmas and protested peacefully in Buttermarket Square, hoping to influence the Church of England to discuss the issue of the rights of divorced fathers to see their children.

Canterbury at War

The Civil War – Canterbury was held by the Parliamentarians and the building that is now Pizza Express was used as a military fort. From the river it is possible to see some discolouration left on the wall by cannon fire. Parliamentary troops in the city were particularly unkind to the cathedral: they used the nave to stable horses, and destroyed the original statue of Christ on the Sanctuary Gate by using it for target practice.

The First World War – The city's main role was as a medical centre for casualties brought from across the Channel. However, the city also had a volunteer regiment, the Buffs, who were particularly prominent in the 3rd Battle of Ypres, after which the *Daily Mail* honoured them with a story on 'The Heroic Men of Kent'.

The Second World War – Advances in aviation since the First World War meant that Canterbury had a very different experience in the 1940s than it had in the previous years of conflict. Westgate Tower was used as a lookout station for German planes, but overall 115 people were killed by bombing in Canterbury, and over 800 ancient buildings were destroyed – most of them medieval. In total, 445 high explosive bombs fell on the city, and around 10,000 fire bombs.

ounded Belgians Canterbury Hospital

The Buffs

The Buffs are otherwise known as the Royal East Kent Regiment, formerly the 3rd Regiment of Foot. Dating back to 1572, this is one of the oldest regiments in the British Army, and third in order of precedence. It existed for almost 400 years, but was disbanded in 1961, and, following various amalgamations, now falls within the Princess of Wales's Royal Regiment.

The Buffs accumulated 116 battle honours, of which four were the Victoria Cross. The winners were:

Frederick Francis Maude, at the time a Major, during the Crimean War. Held his position with only nine or ten men and did not retreat until all hope was lost and he had been dangerously wounded.

John Connors, at the time a Private, in the same. Personally rescued an officer of the 30th Regiment who was surrounded by Russians.

James Smith, a Corporal at the time he won this honour, during the First Mohmand Campaign. His fellow soldiers included a young Winston Churchill. Fought on while wounded and helped other injured men; he then held the line while an officer went for help.

William Richard Cotter, Lance Corporal (acting Corporal), during the First World War. Held his position and supported others while wounded in both arms and with one leg blown off below the knee.

A less favourable view of the Buffs, presumably by someone sympathetic to the competing West Kent Regiment, is preserved in the doggerel rhyme:

The Buffs, the Buffs are going away
Leaving the girls in the family way.
Leaving the Royal West Kent to pay.

Customs and Traditions

Beating the bounds – A ritual in which members of a parish walk around the edges of their area; it began in order to pass on the knowledge of where the boundaries were before maps became common. Although it no longer serves a vital purpose, the practice continues in many areas.

Bumping – A light-hearted part of the 'beating of the bounds' ritual. People are lifted up and dropped gently on to one of the many boundary stones along the route. Local dignitaries like the mayor are usually 'bumped'.

The Hop Hoodening – One of the longest-running festivals celebrating the hop harvest that still goes on. It begins with a procession led by the Hop Queen before a service and performances by country dancers and Morris Men in the cathedral and its precincts. It is accompanied by Hooden Horses, a kind of hobby horse with a snapping jaw: these do not enter the cathedral, because they are a pagan tradition.

Festivals

The Canterbury Festival – An annual festival of music and drama held in October. It was inaugurated in 1929, and has been running in its current form since 1984. Guest artists have ranged from T.S. Eliot and Dorothy Sayers (in the early years) to Alan Bennett, the London Community Gospel Choir and the Chamber Orchestra of Europe more recently. Eliot's *Murder in the Cathedral* was originally written for this event and performed in Canterbury Cathedral.

Anifest – The South East's only animation festival has been running annually since 2007. It includes workshops, performances, talks and awards aimed at everyone from children to industry experts. Subjects of discussion have included Bagpuss, *Wallace & Gromit*, and the dragon from *Harry Potter*.

Catholic Pilgrimage – Annual event organised by the Knights of St Columba in October. Members of the order walk the traditional pilgrimage route while others come to view the procession through the city with the relics of Thomas Becket and the special cathedral service. The event is considerably smaller than it used to be.

Wall Paintings

Pilgrim's Hospital – Has a remarkably well-preserved painting of Christ in Majesty and two of the four evangelists from the late twelfth or early thirteenth century.

Canterbury Museum – Has a sixteenth-century wall painting showing plants. The entire wall from a Tudor building has been removed, moved, and preserved behind glass.

Millennium mural – Painted by Elisa Hudson, this picture details the history of the city and a number of famous people and events associated with it. It runs the full length of the subway near the exit to the bus station. Well worth a look!

Fairtrade shop – The shop on the corner of Palace Street and Orange Street has a door on its first floor that has been painted to look like a woman is waving out of it over a balcony.

Baker – Near the west end of St Peter's Street, where it meets Black Griffin Lane, a baker has been painted on the corner of the first floor.

Painter – On Castle Street, a painted painter is falling off his ladder on the side of a private dwelling.

Sport

Cricket

The Kent County Cricket Club has its headquarters at St Lawrence Grounds in Canterbury. It first came into existence in 1842 and was adapted to the modern form in 1870. During the Second World War, the grounds at St Lawrence were kept up – and an amazing 579 matches were played there, raising money for service charities.

Many of the club's successes came between the years 1967 and 1979: these are known as 'the Glory Years', as eleven trophies were won in this era. In more recent years, the Kent team has made the final of the T20 competition three years in a row (2007-9), and won the trophy in 2007.

Rugby

Canterbury Rugby Club was founded in 1929 and its first skipper was Dudley Hallwood, who became a noted newspaper cartoonist.

Real success did not come until 1974/5, when they won the Kent Cup for the first time, beating Maidstone in the final. The 2005/6 season, the club's most successful, saw them achieving National League status, winning the Kent Cup for the second consecutive year, and being named Team of the Year by *Rugby World* magazine.

Football

The first football team to represent the whole city of Canterbury was set up in 1888, but the first season with an official team was not until 1904. The current club was founded in 1947.

A 'Busby Babe', Mr Bob Harrop was a player and manager of the club for five seasons in the early 1970s.

The team's stadium was redeveloped as housing, and they are in negotiations with Canterbury Council to find a new location; currently they play home matches at Herne Bay's Safety Net Stadium.

Golf

The Canterbury Gold Club was founded in 1926, on land owned by the Ministry of Defence; before that, the land belonged to St Augustine's Abbey. The Abbey connection explains the name 'Scotland Hills': this is a tribute to Scolland (the spelling of which was corrupted over the years, becoming 'Scotland'), the man who was Abbot from 1072.

The course was designed by Harry Colt, a prolific course architect who was involved in the design, construction and modification of 115 courses around the world.

Canterbury Open Week (now renamed the Festival of Golf) in late July has four competitions on consecutive days.

Music

The subgenre of music known as Canterbury Scene or Canterbury Sound is a kind of avant-garde rock with psychedelic and improvisational jazz influences, and often very obscure lyrics. It grew from a group of artists and bands with a connection to the city, though changes in membership over the years mean that the bands now have little geographical coherence.

The main bands were:

Wild Flowers (formed in 1964) – An early influence on the scene, and home, at one time or another, to virtually all the musicians who were to go on to form Caravan and Soft Machine.

Soft Machine (formed in 1966) – Never a great commercial success but generally considered to be one of the most influential bands of the period.

Gong (formed in 1967) – Led by Australian musician David Allen, showing that the Canterbury connection was weak from the start: the group performed at the second Glastonbury festival in 1971.

Caravan (formed in 1968) – Appeared on *Top of the Pops* in 1970 and remained successful in England and abroad well into the 1970s. With various changes of personnel the band is still active in the present day.

Hatfield and the North (formed in 1972) – Made up almost entirely of previous members of other Canterbury Scene bands.

National Health (formed in 1975) – Named after the keyboardist's National Health glasses. Their second record, 'Of Queues and Cures', has been judged the fourth best record of all time on the Gnosis website.

Crab and Winkle Line

The Canterbury–Whitstable Railway (or Crab and Winkle Line) is one of a number of lines that have a claim to be the first passenger railway in the world (1830), but it has an additional claim to fame: the world's first season ticket was issued for travel on it in 1834.

The railway was the idea of engineer William James, and a number of famous early railway engineers were involved in its design and construction – including Joseph Lock, George and Robert Stephenson, and John Rennie.

The original train on the line was *Invicta*, which was built by Robert Louis Stevenson for £635. It was the twentieth train constructed by his company, and was constructed directly after *The Rocket*. The first driver of *Invicta* was Edward Fletcher, who delivered it from Newcastle.

The line declined over the early part of the twentieth century as Whitstable Harbour fell out of use, and consequently there was little demand for the route. It eventually closed in 1952.

The Crab and Winkle Line Trust has existed since 1997. It takes care of the remains of the route, and makes it accessible to the public. In 1999, a footpath and cycleway was opened between Canterbury and Whitstable, running along part of the original track bed.

Future Plans

Beany Museum and Gallery

The old museum, art gallery and city library are being completely refurbished and will be reopened to the public in 2012. While the old high-street frontage will remain the same because it is part of the city's heritage, the interior has been redesigned to double the space available, improve accessibility and provide new activity and educational spaces.

Old Tannery Development

As is the case throughout Kent and the UK, increases in population and changes in lifestyle have led to a demand for more housing. In Canterbury this demand is being met by various projects, one of the largest and most central of which is the development of the site of the old tannery buildings within the city walls.

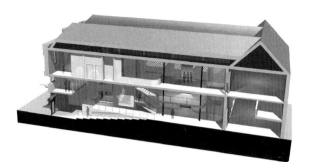

Secret…

On Blackfriars Street, just off King's Street, you can see part of the old Blackfriars' building, which used to be the monastery's refectory. It is now the Cleary Gallery and King's School Art Centre.

St Margaret Street's Waterstones has the remains of a Roman hypocaust from the public baths in its basement, which has been made available to view *in situ* behind glass. The independent café on the top floor is also worth a look.

Greyfriars Chapel and Gardens are on all the tourist information boards and sign posts, but very few people get to them. The quiet, even in the city centre, makes it appealing, and the chapel is interesting architecturally as well.

Must See / Must Do

1. Buy sweets out of jars from one of the many old-fashioned sweet shops, or try the freshly made fudge from the Fudge Kitchen.

2. Take a tour on the river to see the city from a different point of view: fun, informative and a wonderful way to relax.

3. Visit the Museum of Canterbury to see the Rupert Gallery and Oliver Postgate's illustrated life of Thomas Becket.

4. Explore the famous cathedral and its precincts. Visit the tomb of St Thomas, smell the herbs in the Healing Garden and wonder at the splendour of this 1,000-year-old building.

5. Wander through the network of streets surrounding the cathedral. These narrow paths, with towering buildings leaning over them, give the closest impression of what the medieval city would have been like.

6. Relax in one of the city's many gardens and parks. From the tiny Three Cities Garden on Best Lane to the majestic Westgate Gardens, these spaces can provide a moment of calm and peace in a busy day.

7. Take a walk along the medieval city wall, nearly half of which survives, and appreciate the contrast of old and new within this vibrant city.

Online

General

www.canterbury.co.uk
www.canterbury.gov.uk
www.canterburyfestival.co.uk

Attractions

www.canterbury.ac.uk/sidney-cooper
www.canterbury-museums.co.uk
www.canterburywestgatetowers.com
www.eastbridgehospital.org.uk

Tours

www.canterburyrivertours.co.uk
www.canterburypunting.co.uk
www.canterbury-walks.co.uk
www.kent.tours.co.uk

Final facts

The term '**canter**' – a pace in horse-riding – comes from the phrase 'Canterbury Pace', which was the steady speed pilgrims on horseback would go to get through the Westgate.

Charles II stayed at the **Three Tuns Inn** during his journey from Dover to London for his restoration in 1660, after the downfall of Cromwell's Commonwealth government.

The markings on **Whitefriars**' streets are exact recreations of the archaeological notes describing pits found during excavations, enlarged to full size and placed exactly where they were discovered.

Canterbury was the subject of the first ever town history to be published in England, William Somner's 1640 *The Antiquities of Canterbury*, which is still a valuable source for historians.

125

Notes on Illustrations

Image on the cover flap. Westgate Towers by Chas Bedford LRPS